CASTING
FOR THE
CUTTHROAT

CASTING
FOR THE
CUTTHROAT

CHARLES
ENTREKIN

Thunder City Press

1977

Thunder City Press Chapbook No. 6

First Printing   December 1977

ISBN   0-918644-06-2

ACKNOWLEDGEMENTS

Grateful acknowledgement is made to the following magazines, in which some of these poems have or will appear: BERKELEY'S POETS' COOPERATIVE, AURA, US 1.

"Missoula Spring" first appeared with the back photo as a People Poems Poster in Oakland, California. Reprinted with permission.

for Richard Hugo

CASTING FOR THE CUTTHROAT

He sneaks after some woman who could not love him,
a woman from his school days, who would never love him.
He knew it, sneaking like a thief after the praise
from her lips, like a fisherman casting
only for the cutthroat, living
out his years forever dumb
before this woman who could touch him,
thinking only the barrenness of Garnet,
Montana could cure him,
this madness that could not be cured,
his own special madness,
the way the green of a river bank
reminds him of her,
the way she's always young as porcelain
and he's grown old, his books
like school houses ablaze in the snow.

MASTERS

I pick you out, a man to become,
yes and no together; you lead me
into the desert. Your single words
are too thick for meaning. I
can't make them out. The cactus
plants are all I understand. And
the heat.
    In the moment I look around
you fall behind: whose death
do I feel? This is all a dream.
I wake, think of writing it down.
A man walks in thru my window
from Montana. "Thirty white geese
are saved from extinction," he says,
helps himself to my liquor.
We ignore the snow.
    "I was just in Mexico," I said,
did you feel something die?" He rages out
in the midst of a blizzard, with my liquor.
This is another dream. They flower
like carnations in a bowl. The white petals
all sink to the ground in a row.

EXPECTATIONS

    And what could be done
has been done to her. An acid rain
falls over New York; and as you sleep
a white, day-light moon seems to speak,
saying,
    take these dreams, shiny and bald
as they are, no expectations turn
as she turns.
    But no matter the words in your throat
you wake to a gray covered day, the whisper
of dawn rain, and it fills you with the sound
of weeping, with the sorrow that comes
when you don't know what's wrong.

XXI   THE WORLD, REVERSED

Now,
old refusals come out of the ground like swords;
they went unrecognized for years.

I watch the freeway traffic and think of home,
not the real one, but the one I imagined
where failures were forgotten.

I have weaved the clothes of a castaway
believing expectations I filled
would fulfill my needs.

How easy to continue even when it's wrong,
when momentum carries me like sleep;
and I need only to quit,

to sit silent
with one word
brewing in my mouth.

A FALSE RESPONSE, 1976

for Michael Covino

When you asked about the absence
of artifacts in our poems, I said,
because they no longer last, like plastic bags,
like water vapor on the moon, I said,
yes they are gone, separated from us,
because price and population have become
the involucrums of our artifacts.
But I was wrong. Tonight those words
seem quick and false, like dust from the wake
of what's gone, like a simulation of thought.
The question was wrong. The answer was wrong.
Only death is real, and the inarticulate sounds
that grow into song, the ceaseless flowering
of what's living that will not be stopped.
And I think of the thirst of the dead,
how their wanting came to nothing; but lives on,
the wanting that runs underground, surrounding
like a distant voice in my ear.

THOUGHTS FROM A PLANE OVER BIRMINGHAM

My mother sick, the plane drifts
years, banking for landing, and suddenly
I'm home,
and the orange, industrialized sky
still says the furnaces are working overtime,
steel from the steel-born town.
The stewardess shakes the sleepers awake,
the engines rev, landing gear down, and the home
I thought I'd left behind returns
as we touch the ground. Home
because what opens at the beginning remains
open till the end.

ADVANTAGE

In France beside some shabby old wall
the water runs dirty with sunlight
and I walk, moss-brown stones beneath my feet,
toward you with open arms.   You are blond now.
You have changed only the color of your hair.
All the rest remains the same.
        In your eyes I see you don't understand,
as if you're puzzled by my greeting.   Being polite
you invite me to coffee before finding you're afraid:
there are no witnesses.   Always we are alone.
It's then you begin to doubt, and I discover
once again how your grave face will unravel,
        remembering when we were young,
when your dark hair glistened like a river in the sun.

HIGH, ALL-NIGHT DRIVING TO BERKELEY

Drink beer, follow the headlights,
the highway knows where a woman waits
who loves me.   Drunks pass on by;
all maniacs stay in bed; I'm high
and Berkeley's near with its strong
ocean-like ways.   The desert behind, a song
plays in my ear.   Already sea waves run white
lines one at a time down the moon-lit night.
Your tides pull me along; your curve of thigh
runs in my mind; your round brown eyes
close once again.   Take me, take me, says the song;
the maps show I can make no wrong
decisions.   Home, to know your body as before;
I am a desert wrecked dreamer come to shore.

MISSOULA SPRING

I have become
one of my own poems.
This morning
the covered streets
opened black
in melting snow.
    I was wrong.
Winter gone, a flower
opens in me, a song, words
crawl in my veins,
a carnation of the brain,
a dogwood.

FOR ROBIN GREGG, 19

*Today, counts of dirt particles reached 400
microgram per cubic meter.*
BIRMINGHAM NEWS
July 23, 1976

In Birmingham
there is a kind of sleep
that comes up like a bank of fog
that says there is no point
to getting up
because there is no point to it;
it claims young men
sleeping in garages,
heart shutting down
for lack of air.

CARPE DIEM

You can't find your shoes
      Exiting your closet as from the insides
of a civilization you stand in the ruins:
all the etcetera of a lifetime: your huge
British cadillac of a baby carriage, slide
projector, vacuum cleaner, umbrella...
      but not the shoes you need.
      You enter the bathroom without looking back,
slip into a hot tub of water. Your eyes seethe
brown with wickedness over your body. The suds
have crept to your hair.
      With a breath, your breasts float high
in the gray water.
     : You are alive.
      You become, slowly, the woman's body
you understand, your own, and
      you know when you step from the tub,
wet and warm-red, with
      pieces of dreams still molten inside you,
      how porcelain your world can become.

for Maggie in Berkeley

THIS STILLNESS

As she goes up the stairs, suddenly
I remember a river I once watched
rushing powerful and dark after a long rain.
Her shoulders seem thin and spare.
I stare at her thighs softly splotched
with white paint. Two canvases tonight.
Fatigue rests in her eyes. She says good night.
Overhead a jet rumbles through the dark,
cars pass in the street. I listen as she undresses.
The children sleep. And I remember the river:
how it seemed strangely unfamiliar, becoming
a remorseless, ceaseless roar, taking everything
within its reach; and I sat beside it on the bank, arms
around my knees, holding this stillness inside me.

ALL THOSE WOMEN WANTING TO DIE

No longer takes me by surprise.
    The heavy magic of dreamers
sometimes self-destructs; only their words
are left behind.   The body floats away,
    a black coach in January air, a wind
over coastal mountains, returning home,
zephers, ciphers,
    like frail shadows
before the light goes out.

THE DISAPPEARANCE OF JOHN

A young woman is working over her husband.
He's becoming a statue. She hammers away, shouting,
"John, John, I know you can hear me. John?"
But even as she hammers, he's slipping
into stone. He is not escaping, he knows,
the blood is ceasing to flow, replaced
bit by bit by stone.
Already his eyes appear to be fading,
that feverish glow of anxiety gone. "John?
Are you in there?" and the chisel in haste
placed just center of the shoulder blades,
"John?"
Staring at the resultant dust
on her kitchen floor, she stamps her foot,
"John, this has gone too far!"
before she sweeps him up, and stores
what remains in a silver jar.

THE SEPARATION

It happened a sleepless evening after one of her parties, as though she'd been waiting for him. She felt strangely deserted, her husband asleep, the servants gone, and her house seemed to vibrate like a tuning fork set below the range of human hearing. A wind had come up. She paced the floors, listening, and suddenly he was there. Young. Blonde. The feel of an abandoned child in his eyes, the slight fuzz of a beard on his cheeks.

At first she wanted to call the police, but she couldn't bring herself to do it. Light seemed to gather around his face. A new feeling rose inside her. As though she'd taken a lover. And so he remained. She allowed it.

From behind the lace curtains of her upstairs window, she watched him pee into the gardenia bush. It was the simplicity of his acts, she decided, that fascinated her so. Secretly, she mapped the range and the hour of his small excursions into her garden. She knew what he ate, when and where he relieved himself. The smallest of his movements took on an exaggerated importance. To know he was on the grounds was a comfort she could not explain. Something about him called out to her.

It was early one cold morning, a light snow on the ground, she began to worry about him. A darkness gathered in his face. He seemed suddenly somewhat emaciated. True, lately, she had ignored him, but.... it occurred to her she should go down to him. She couldn't bring herself to do it.

That evening she dreamed she stood over a pool of stagnant water, stirred with a thick stick, lazy brown goldfish, each with the face of her child. All slowly dying. She woke up screaming.

Her nightgown raised to her knees, she ran out to him.

His face had become like chalk. His eyes were empty.

She kneeled beside him, almost touched him, and for the first time he seemed about to speak. She leaned closer.

His mouth fell open with a sudden bright flaming. A wind rushed over them. The house watched them lift from the ground. Lace curtains reached out for her. Her husband sat up in his bed. The echo of her name banged through his empty house.

SPRING LETTER TO DONALD PHELPS

(with love and for your bad handwriting)

First opened your letter several days ago;
small tatters of words still fall out
unrecognized, and at night I feel presences,
predatory shapes at my window, and sad animals
hurt greatly, returning home in the dark.
It's in their eyes.

    Last evening I read it again, and again
could make out only the good parts. Comes clear
like some piece of news read thru blurred print,
yesterday's paper unwrapped from a fine trout dinner.
It's good. I trust you. Intuit what you say.

    This spring brings a drought they tell us
though it's rained two weeks straight; only a spring
rain, they say, too little too late. Even so
I feel afloat in a great gray, forever green
and foggy land. The drought seems only in the news.

    Living here makes me want to cry out
like an Aztec, "Hey! Lifegiver, how come you so shy?
Why don't you talk to us?"

    But it's spring and once again the business men
have returned from the slopes. Broken limbs.
Beautiful tans.

    Sometimes I feel I have no instincts here,
no voice for the absence of seasons. I want to hide
in alleyways, but soldiers hide there, eyes gone inward,
no legs; toss one a quarter and two old men rise
from garbage cans, strike at the silver color.

Tonight I want only to hide on the dark side
of words, no need to understand, and flee
with the animals from some black shape
at home in this forever green land.
Thank you for your letter about my book.

Charles

LETTER TO ROD TULLOSS

Poets who are clerks? computer programmers?
taxmen? auditors? I know of no poets who fit these
job classifications. It's not a matter of how you earn
your living, but what comes first and how much time
you allow for it. True, the reality of working for a
living does not ring with that subtle quality of academic
laughter. It's a wordless occupation that leaves no
room for anyone but the young and the aged. There
was school and that meant you should learn as much
as you could because life was a rich and variously
complex web and you could wind up making a bad end-
ing of it. It meant that somehow all of the parts re-
lated to a whole and you could make sense of it if you
tried. Then one day you graduated and you had to
have a job. And you discover you are not living in
Ancient Greece. No. You are living in and through
the Fall of the Roman Empire. It's worse than you
thought: working every day, two days off out of
every seven. Two days yours. Seven days theirs.
And it doesn't make any sense. Even though the
work has its good moments. It's because you be-
lieve in choices. Riches. Material possessions.
Not enough to be warm and healthy and clothed. The
need to found yourself in some thing. A house. The
future of your children. Every day. Until you're
old. Sixty. And can no longer perform adequately.
Make mistakes. Your brain no longer receives an

abundant supply of oxygen; your blood is old. And then you get a pension. The freedom to be whatever you want to make of your one-third salary for the rest of your life.

But even so it makes no difference. It's what comes first. And if you must divide your life, how many parts can there be before you lose a sense of the whole and fall into bitterness.

I walk down the streets of Berkeley, past the spot where last night a man was shot three times, in the chest, in the side, in the arm, telling me, "I'm shot up pretty bad I think....I don't know who they were, never saw them before in my life...", the blood filling the insides of his shirt, and now there is a yellow arrow on the curb pointing to where he was lying and in the sky there are heavy white clouds that remind me of snow and I think of going to Montana.

Look for us in September.

Charles

Charles Entrekin was born in Birmingham in 1941, received his B. A. from Birmingham Southern College and M. F. A. from the University of Montana. He now lives in Berkeley where he helped found the Berkeley Poets Cooperative. His stories and poems have appeared in many small press publications and he is also the author of ALL PIECES OF A LEGACY.

*   *   *

Printed in Birmingham, Alabama, October, 1977. Cover design and artwork by Maggie Entrekin for the Thunder City Press. Back photo by David Curry from People Poems, a series of posters that appeared in Oakland, California. Reprinted with permission. Book design by Steven Ford Brown and Sandra S. Thompson. This edition is a limited first printing of 500 copies; 25 copies numbered and signed by the author.